One Direction

The Story So Far

Mason Crest

Contents

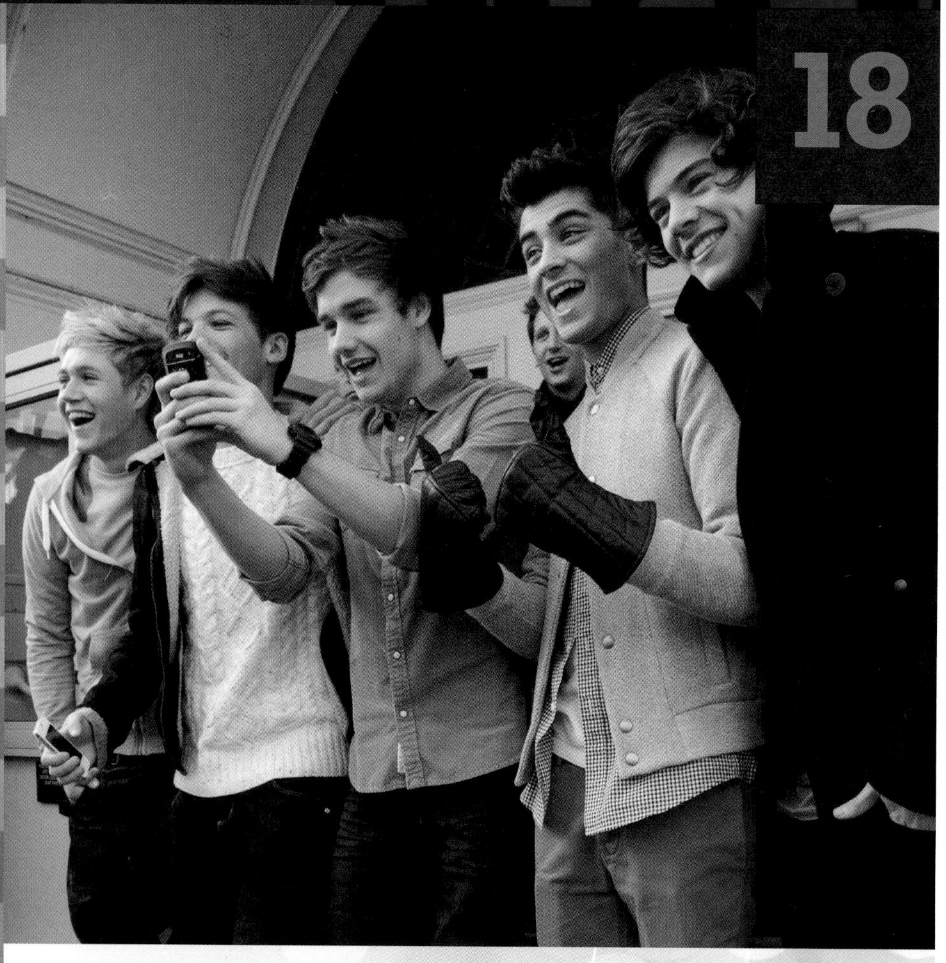

Mason Crest
450 Parkway Drive, Suite D
Broomall, PA 19008
www.masoncrest.com

Printed and bound in the United States of America.

10 9 8 7 6 5 4 3 2 1

Cataloging-in-Publication Data on file with the Library of Congress.

ISBN: 978-1-4222-3249-1
ebook ISBN: 978-1-4222-8662-3

Written by: Holly French

Images courtesy of PA Photos, Shutterstock and Mirrorpix

Introduction

"I went to the One Direction concert in Auckland, New Zealand. It was honestly the best night of my life! I thought I would lose my voice and be deaf. They were amazing and there were some extremely dedicated fans. I ♥ One Direction!"

Rachael Sawyers, 14, New Zealand

Five talented boys, with one common dream: to make it to the top in the music industry. This is the story of Harry, Zayn, Liam, Louis, and Niall, who all auditioned as individual competitors for *The X Factor* in 2010 and formed the boy band One Direction – aka 1D – under the guidance of the British television show. Thanks to talent, hard work, social media, and the popularity of the show and its live tour, this British-Irish boy band has proved that they have what it takes to reach the top of the charts.

The X Factor was in its seventh season when the UK's newest pop icons first appeared on screen. From five young guys who didn't know each other, One Direction quickly established themselves as an up-and-coming band and now has an impressive devoted fan base of Directioners, a #1 debut single, "What Makes You Beautiful", and the debut album "Up All Night", which started at #2 on the UK

Albums Chart and became the fastest-selling debut album of 2011 in the UK. In the US it did even better and it debuted at #1. This epic rise made One Direction the first UK group in history to hit the top spot on the US Billboard 200 with a debut album! This news in March 2012 followed the group's success at the UK's BRIT Awards in February when "What Makes You Beautiful" beat favorite, Adele, to the coveted Best British Single. Their second album, "Take Me Home," was released in November 2012.

The boys had all wanted solo careers before they found fame with One Direction on *The X Factor* and although it began the start of an exciting rise to fame for each of them, they gave everything they had, built up lasting friendships and working relationships, and helped to make the show a real success in 2010. These five boys made the show extremely popular that year and helped to establish it and One Direction beyond the shores of the UK and Ireland. Boy bands had been fading on the chart scene for a few years, but a crop of British bands including The Wanted and now, One Direction, have changed all that and boy bands look like they're here to stay. Appearing on *The X Factor* gave the boys an instant fan base from which to build on and they know that their fans are the ones who have helped them get where they are today. Follow the success...

■ **RIGHT:** One Direction (L-R) Liam Payne, Louis Tomlinson, Harry Styles, (with mentor Simon Cowell), Zayn Malik, and Niall Horan during *The X Factor* Press Conference, 2010.

Harry Styles

Biographies

Harry Styles, the youngest and possibly one of the most popular members of 1D, has a very proud family! He is very close to both his mother and his sister Gemma, and the family miss Harry when he's busy working. The family lived in Evesham, Worcestershire, when Harry was born in February 1994, but they soon moved to Holmes Chapel in Cheshire where he grew up, went to Happy Days nursery and attended Holmes Chapel Comprehensive School – which is now an Academy and Specialist Science College.

When Harry was seven his parents Anne and Des divorced and he moved with his mom and Gemma away from Holmes Chapel to a bar, which Anne managed. It was a sad time for Harry and his sister because their mom and dad weren't together anymore, but he does have good memories of being a kid, like when the family went to Disney World. He even remembers his first day at school and that he settled there pretty quickly. He enjoyed performing in school plays and his first ever performance was as a toy – Buzz Lightyear – in the toy shop while the children in *Chitty Chitty Bang Bang* were hiding from the child catcher. But, his first singing solo came when he played a mouse called Barney!

Harry has always loved singing and his dad, Des Styles, introduced him to music. He became a fan of Elvis through listening to his dad's music and recorded a number of Elvis tracks with his cousin on a karaoke machine. Harry was also good at math from a young age, but preferred English as he grew older. Like other members of the band, Harry is a keen soccer player and enjoyed sports at school. He was popular at school and had lots of friends. When he was 12, he moved back to Holmes Chapel with his family and his mom remarried. Harry was happy when his mother met Robin Twist and was really pleased when they decided to get married. Harry had his first proper girlfriend when he was 12; Emilie is still Harry's friend today. Despite the fact that Harry's mom and stepdad were a big part of his life – he has called himself a mommy's boy! – he is also very close to his dad who is just as supportive and proud of Harry as Anne and Gemma are. Harry and his sister have had the usual ups and downs that siblings often have, but they have always been close and Gemma spends as much time with Harry as she can even though she's away studying at Sheffield University. While One Direction were in the live shows on *The X Factor* Gemma traveled down to London every weekend to support the band.

Although Harry had his moments messing around at school he did really well in his GCSE examinations and his family are also proud of all his other talents – like juggling! Harry's hair – for which he's well known – started to go really curly when he was 12. No one in the family knows why it did; Gemma has straight hair and mom Anne's is wavy. He is quite competitive and enjoyed badminton – like his dad – at school where he played the sport quite a bit. The skill and the challenge needed for badminton appealed to Harry but he became seriously interested in music when he formed a band with some guys from school, Will (his best friend), Nick, and Hayden. The boys entered a Battle of the Bands competition at school with their band, White Eskimo. The band won the competition and went on to become really good, playing at events. It was the motivation Harry needed and although he was nervous he applied for *The X Factor*.

Biographies

Zayn Malik

Born in Bradford in 1993, Zayn Malik comes from a big family and he has lots of aunts, uncles, and cousins. The family is close and Zayn is pleased to have so many supportive people around him. But, life hasn't always been that easy for the popular member of One Direction and when he was younger, he found that he didn't "fit" at his two earliest schools because of his mixed race heritage – Zayn's mom Tricia is English and his dad Yaser is British Pakistani. Despite life being difficult to start with at school, Zayn enjoyed looking after his three sisters, Doniya (who is older than him), Waliyha, and Safaa. He also liked to perform to his family whenever he could. He readily admits that he was quite hyperactive as a child and was a bit of a handful for his family (especially his mom), and sugar was a big trigger that sent him bouncing off the walls!

Zayn settled in at school in East Bowling, Bradford, where he joined the choir. He loved performing and landed the main role in *Bugsy Malone*. He was good at English and had a reading age much higher than his years. He sat his GCSE in English a year early and got an A, but he wasn't so keen on math when he attended Tong High School in Bradford.

Of all the boys, Zayn is probably the most private. He takes his time getting to know people and only "lets in" those he feels really close to. He first started thinking about his image when he was around 12 and still takes great pride in his hair! He loved school plays and drama in general, and landed a part in *Grease* where he enjoyed being able to be a different character. At this time, singing wasn't as important for Zayn but when asked to join the choir he happily went along. He readily admits that he was quite short until he went to high school, and he was known to have stood on a brick to kiss a girl! He didn't have a proper girlfriend until he was about 15 and he has only had a few relationships since including one with fellow *X Factor* contestant, Perrie Edwards from girl band Little Mix. Zayn really misses his mom now that he is based in London, but they call each other all the time on the phone so that they can catch up on both what Zayn is up to and what his family is doing. Zayn is a good laugh, but he can also be a little bit moody at times. Zayn might have become an actor, like his mate Aquib Khan, if it hadn't been for *The X Factor.* But, a music teacher at his school persuaded Zayn to audition for the show. He had an application form twice (when he was 15 and again when he was 16), but didn't fill it out until he was 17. He almost didn't go to the audition because he was too nervous. Thanks to his mom, Zayn finally made it to the audition and was amazed when he made it through to the next stages. He was worried about being rejected, and couldn't quite believe that he kept getting put through.

Zayn's audition as an individual candidate on *The X Factor* wasn't broadcast in 2010 but was shown after the season ended on the spin-off show, *The Xtra Factor*. He found Boot Camp very hard and suffered from nerves, especially when he was expected to dance. He even stayed backstage on one occasion and could have been eliminated. Thankfully, he made it through and is now one of the most popular members of One Direction.

Biographies

Liam Payne

Liam Payne arrived in the world with underlying problems and a dysfunctional kidney when he was born three weeks early in Wolverhampton in 1993. It was a worrying time for his parents Karen and Geoff and his two older sisters Ruth and Nicola, but even though one kidney eventually packed up for good, Liam fought back and is now a great member of One Direction. Up until he was four, Liam had to have regular tests due to his condition – the hospital couldn't find out what was wrong – and he suffered a great deal of pain. This meant that he had to have a large number of injections every day, but at the age of five, he sang his first karaoke solo at a holiday camp. It probably wasn't his best performance, but it gave him a taste for being on stage performing and it was something he liked to do whenever he could. At school, Liam wasn't the best of pupils and messed about quite a bit and he was often called in to see the head teacher, but he excelled at cross-country and he took the training very seriously. He would get up at 6.00am to run and by the age of 12 was running in the school's under-18s team. Liam then joined an athletics club and became the third best 1,500 meters runner for his age in the country – a huge achievement. He ran for the UK but failed to gain a place in the England Schools team. He was 14 years old and decided to concentrate on his singing. But he did join the basketball team at high school. However, because he had some great gear he'd bought in the US he was picked on by some of the older kids at school. As a result of the bullying, Liam took up boxing in order to defend himself and ended up with quite a few injuries! But, what it did do was give Liam confidence and he was able to take on the bullies at school and he won a fight (which he would rather not have had to fight). Liam also joined the performing arts group, Pink Productions, along with his sisters. At the same time, Liam was eager to get himself into business and began selling sweets to kids at school based on his experiences of watching the TV show *Dragons' Den,* which helps budding entrepreneurs. This was how he made his money because a Saturday job was out of the question due to the singing gigs he did at the time. He went to college to study music technology and he loved singing and dancing. He really liked to sing former Take That star Robbie Williams' songs, especially at karaoke, and as a very young child he did a good impression of Liam Gallagher, from UK band Oasis, in his dad's sunglasses!

Liam has always got on really well with his sisters Nicola and Ruth and says that Ruth is very like him: both like to sing! Although Liam decided at a young age to concentrate on his music rather than his sport, like Harry, he loves soccer and played at school whenever he could and used to go to see West Bromwich Albion matches. He was never really into fashion when he was growing up and even went to his audition on *The X Factor* with a hole in his shoe, and unlike some of his band mates, his hair is not as important. He's even considering shaving it off! Liam auditioned for the show for the first time for the fifth season in 2008. He did well, but Simon Cowell felt that he needed more time and asked the then 14-year-old to come back in two years. Liam would have tried again for the sixth season in 2009, but he narrowly missed out when the producers of the show raised the minimum age limit from 14 to 16. But, Liam was back in front of the judges in 2010 having waited in a queue for nine hours!

Louis Tomlinson

Chatty is how Louis Tomlinson has been since he learned to talk. Born in Doncaster in December 1991 he's the oldest member of 1D and started singing at the young age of five. Louis discovered that he was sociable when he started at nursery school in his hometown and fell in love with Power Rangers! Louis' family moved to Poole in Dorset, which he loved. He was a happy kid growing up by the sea, which was made all the more special with the Power Rangers rides on the seafront! He started school at Uplands in Poole and his younger sister Charlotte was born. The family then moved back to Doncaster and he went to Willow Primary School. Félicité and twins Daisy and Phoebe followed Louis and Charlotte, and although he adores his sisters, Louis would have liked to have had a little brother. But, a house full of women has taught him a great deal and he loves kids and babies. Growing up, Louis was close to his grandparents, Edna and Len, and loved having a big family. (In case you're wondering, Louis would like a big family of his own one day.)

Louis began to take his singing seriously at the age of 14, which turned out to be a crazy time for him at school. He ended up changing high schools twice, which was a bit disruptive, and he didn't really settle when he attended Hall Cross. When Louis was offered a place at another local school, Hayfield, he took the chance to move, but found it hard because all the other kids had already made friends. He was 13 at the time, but eventually he settled and made great new friends. Louis began performing at school and joined the band, The Rogue. Geoff, Stan, Jona, and Jamie asked Louis if he'd like to try out as their singer (even though they hadn't heard him sing) and he soon settled into rehearsals once a week. He also sang at school in the end-of-term performance and landed the part of Danny Zuko in the school production of *Grease*. Being in the band gave Louis confidence and he started to enter local talent competitions, while the play gave him the chance to showcase his acting and singing abilities.

Louis also had a part as an extra because when Daisy and Phoebe had roles as babies on a TV drama called *Fat Friends,* he would go along. This led Louis to an acting school and more small parts on TV. Louis went back to school for further studies, and he had a job at the toy store Toys R Us, as well as doing some work experience at Barnsley Soccer Club. He'd failed his first year of A-level examinations and the decision was made to move to college. This may have seemed tough at the time, but here Louis was able to star in a number of musical productions.

At the time Louis auditioned for *The X Factor* he was studying for his AS-level examinations in English Literature, Physical Education, and A2 Theater Studies. After One Direction made it to the live shows he was too busy rehearsing to go back to college and while he could still go back if he wanted, nobody is really expecting he will! Louis' parents, Johanna and Mark Tomlinson, separated in 2011.

Louis did well in his first audition in front of the judges and was given votes by all three, but he was rejected at Boot Camp and asked if he'd like to be part of One Direction. Apparently the boys were given about five minutes to make up their minds. All five said yes and One Direction was born. Louis shared a luxury batchelor pad in London with Harry before moving back to Doncaster while he decides where to base himself next.

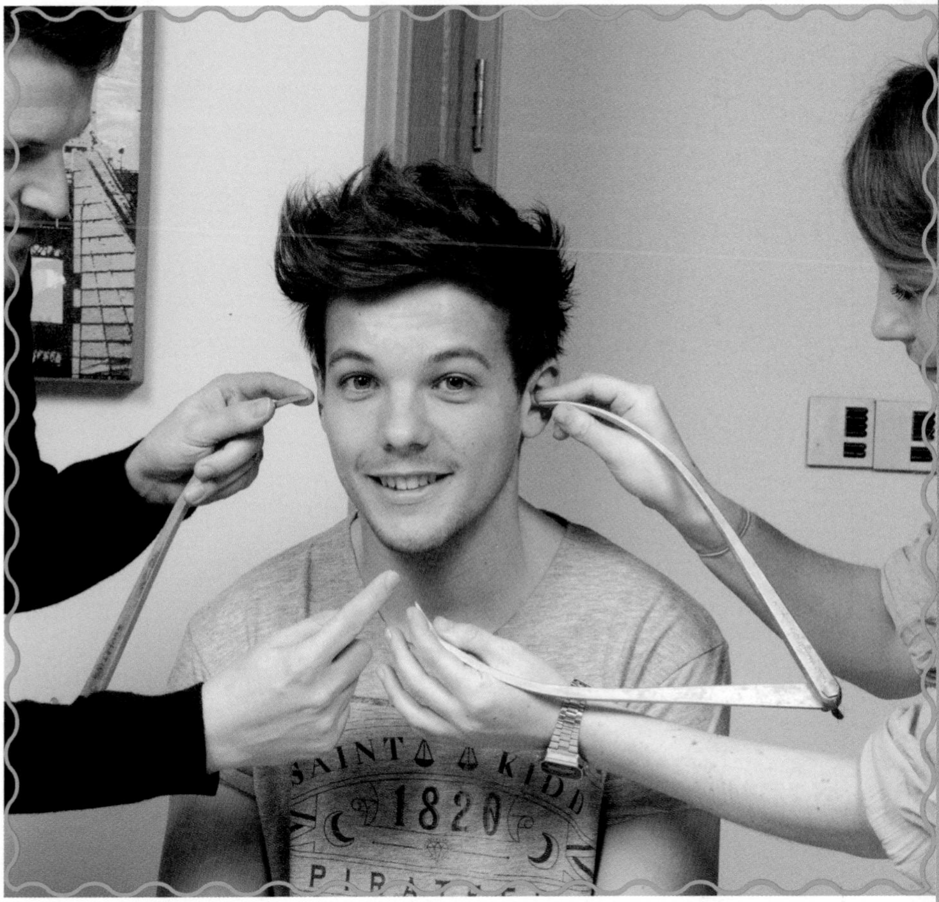

Biographies

Niall Horan

Niall Horan is known as the cheeky member of 1D! Born in Ireland in 1993, the smiley member of the band grew up in the small town of Mullingar in County Westmeath. Like the other members of One Direction he began singing at an early age and by the time he was eight, showed real talent. A teacher at school advised Niall to take his singing seriously and at the age of 10 he took the lead role in a school production of *Oliver*. The young Irish lad found that being on stage made him happy and he also joined the school choir. He especially enjoyed singing at Christmas and kept up playing his guitar (he loves his guitar and thinks it's the best Christmas present he ever had). Niall began singing and acting at the Mullingar Arts Centre and entered all the talent shows at his school.

But it wasn't all plain sailing for Niall. When he was five, his parents, Maura and Bobby, decided to separate and Niall and his older brother Greg lived with their mom for a while before a few years of living in both their parent's houses. Eventually, Niall decided to live with his dad, Bobby, because he lived in town and it made it easier for the budding performer to get together with his friends where he could hang out, have a laugh, and mess about a bit. Niall's first confidence in his abilities came at the age of 12 when he performed "The Man Who Can't Be Moved" by The Script at a school talent show. The event was well covered in the local press and it gave him enough motivation to enter a competition with his friend, Kieron (who accompanied him on the guitar). Niall won the competition and decided that perhaps his singing was OK! He continued to enter competitions and shows and in 2009 he entered the Mullingar Shamrocks' show called Stars In Their Eyes. Niall did really well at impersonating Jason Mraz singing "I'm Yours" and the audience went wild. It showed Niall that he had the potential to be something special and he supported Lloyd Daniels (a contestant on *The X Factor* in 2009) and decided that he could also audition for the show. Immediately after Joe McElderry won *The X Factor* show in December, Niall registered for an audition. He knew what he wanted… to be a professional singer. Back home Niall has often been compared to Justin Bieber which is something he has never minded. Niall is confident in who he is and what his talents and abilities are, and while waiting for his audition on the show entertained fellow contestants with his singing and guitar playing to Bieber's "One Time." Niall was a schoolboy hoping to make it big when he auditioned on *The X Factor* and despite the three votes out of four, there were mixed reviews from the judges. Long-time judge Louis Walsh was particularly in favor of Niall and he made it through to Boot Camp. It must have been hard for him when he didn't make it through to the boys' category on the show, but then, if he had, things would have been very different!

Niall didn't always get on that well with his older brother Greg; both boys found the other annoying. Greg hated that Niall wanted to hang out with all his much older mates, while Niall hated it if Greg even looked at him! Brothers!! But, when Niall was around 13, Greg left school and got a job and the two started to find that they liked each other really. Now Niall and Greg are friends as well as brothers and they don't fight like they used to. If Niall hadn't done well on *The X Factor* he had planned to study sound engineering at university but like the other boys he was given the chance to be in 1D. Fab news for Directioners everywhere!!

Five become One (Direction)

When Harry, Zayn, Liam, Louis, and Niall turned up to audition for *The X Factor* they all had high hopes of success. All five boys had proved in their lives before the show that they had talent and they could sing. They were all hoping for something positive to come out of the experience that they were about to go through. They all wanted to get through to the auditions in front of the judges, but none of them can have known just how dramatically their lives were about to change forever!

Harry, Zayn, Liam, Louis, and Niall all registered for the auditions as solo performers and didn't even know each other. They came from various parts of the UK while Niall auditioned at Croke Park in Dublin, Ireland. But, that wasn't the end of it! He had to have two auditions in front of staff on the show before he was finally (over a month later) seen by Simon Cowell, Louis Walsh, Cheryl Cole, and Katy Perry. Niall's audition gave him mixed reviews from the judges and two of them were unsure of his abilities. However, Louis Walsh was sure that Niall was right for live shows and he eventually came away from his first audition with three votes out of four from the judges. His audition of "So Sick" by Ne-Yo was shown on *The Xtra Factor* and not the main show, and Niall was potentially on the road to success. One of the first to audition was Louis who found himself in front of the judges in Manchester. His audition wasn't shown on the

■ **ABOVE:** Louis Walsh – *X Factor* judge and prominent boy band manager. He has had huge success with Irish bands Westlife and Boyzone in the past.

show and neither was Zayn's. The boy from Bradford was so nervous that he almost didn't make it to his audition. Thanks to his mom though, Zayn had his moment in front of the judges. Harry also auditioned in Manchester singing "Isn't She Lovely" by Stevie Wonder and it was shown on the main show. His talent shone through; he was an instant hit with the audience (often a tough crowd) and many fans of *The X Factor*, as well as the producers, thought he had a good chance of making it to the live shows. Liam possibly had the toughest job of all. The judges had rejected him before – he'd made it to Judges' Houses – and he needed to prove to Simon Cowell that he had what it took to

■ **LEFT:** Simon Cowell – judge and mentor.

■ **BELOW:** Celebrity *X Factor* judge Katy Perry has her picture taken with fans; she was there for Niall's audition in Dublin.

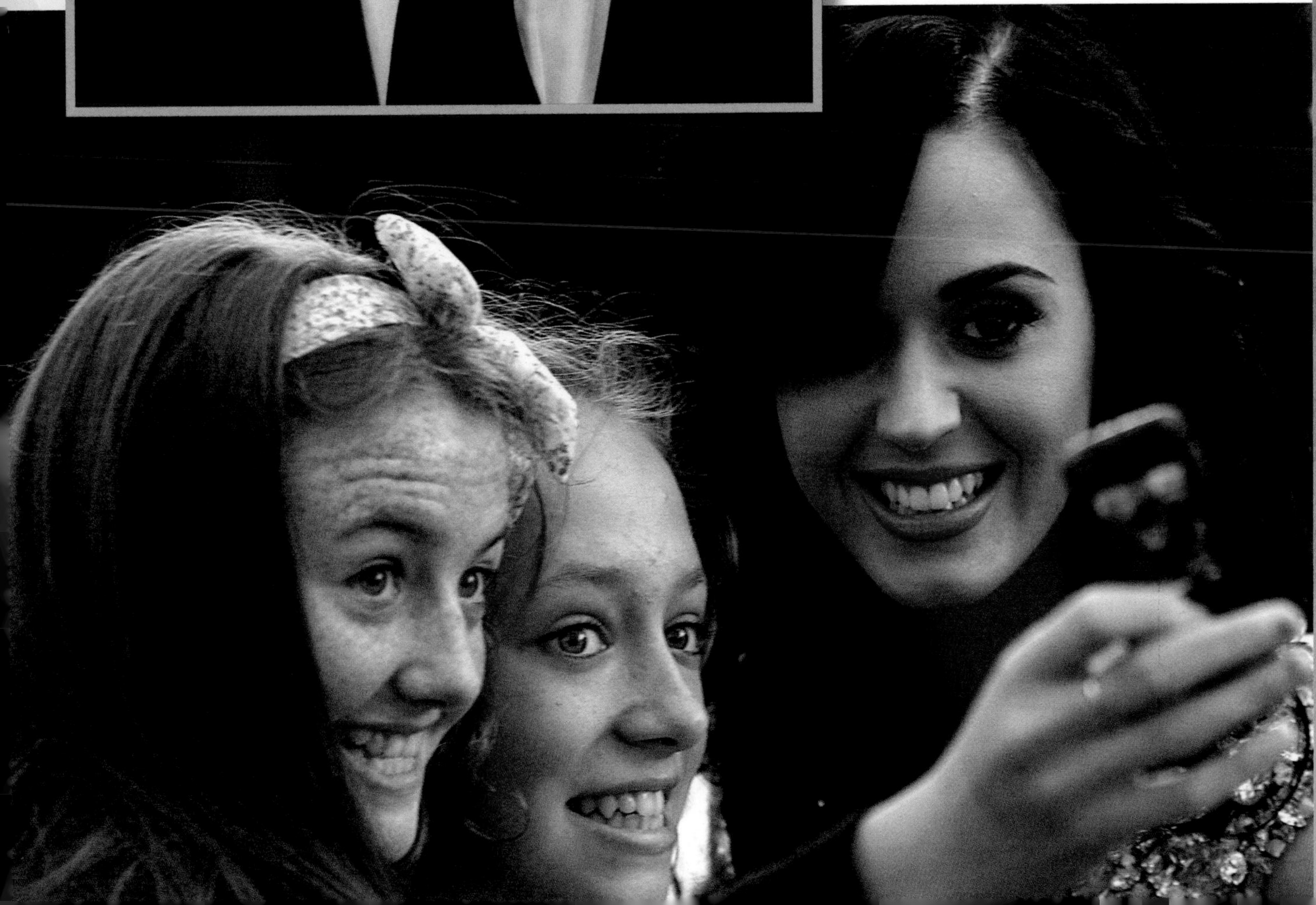

be a star performer. Singing the blues, "Cry Me A River," the whole crowd were on their feet cheering and shouting before he had even finished! Liam has a very powerful voice, which was noted by the judges who all voted in favor of Liam going through. For all five boys, the first round was over, but there was still so much more to prove.

Boot Camp is a tough five days, which the boys experienced at Wembley Arena in July 2010. This is the show's way of deciding who of the remaining acts will make it through to Judges' Houses. In season seven, there were 211 acts who made it to Boot Camp and they were divided into groups of Boys, Girls, Groups and the Over-25s (but a suggestion from Nicole Scherzinger later changed this to the Over-28s). Harry, Zayn, Liam, Louis, and Niall were all hoping to get into the boys category. It was the first time the five had met and

■ **BELOW:** Brian Friedman helped to choreograph the boys' routines on the show.

their first challenge was to sing "Man In The Mirror" by Michael Jackson. It was a nervous time for all five boys; half of all the boys would be going home at the end of day one! The boys were warned that there would be no second chances…

They all made it through to day two, where they were expected to dance under the guidance of Brian Friedman, the show's choreographer. This was where it got really tough for Zayn who stayed backstage because he'd never danced before. It was the first time that the show had introduced dancing at Boot Camp and he was nervous about dancing in front of the cameras, the judges, and the other contestants! He even stated on camera that he didn't want to appear like a fool and he couldn't do it. This could have meant that Zayn's dreams were over before they even began, but Simon Cowell recognized that he had something special and was keen to give the boy from South Yorkshire another chance. He persuaded Zayn to give the dancing a go and although Zayn found it very hard, he did at least try in the end.

Day three saw Nicole Scherzinger arrive in place of Cheryl Cole who was really ill at the time. It was Nicole who was going to change the boys' lives! They had to choose from a list of songs to perform in front of the judges.

Nicole had already worked as a judge on the show and was keen to be back making the important decision about who would make it to Judges' Houses. As Cheryl was ill and the other female judge, Australian singer Dannii Minogue, (who was expecting a baby), couldn't be at Boot Camp, for the first time, it was decided that the "live" audience show would be cancelled during the week. It was another nervous day for the boys who had no idea after their individual performances whether they had made it through or not. On the final day of Boot Camp there were 30 nervous boys standing on stage waiting to hear if they were through. Unfortunately for all five none of them were picked to be put through to the next stage.

Harry, Zayn, Liam, Louis, and Niall were really upset. They were teary and unbelieving as they made their way off the stage. They were all heading for home with their hearts in their boots when they were called back on stage along with four of the girls. It had been Nicole's idea to form two groups. The nine singers that stood back in front of the judges were just too good to let go. The news that if they agreed to become a group meant they would go to Judges' Houses stunned the boys. Liam was the only one who really needed to think about it (but he only had

■ **ABOVE:** Zayn lines up in auditions with fellow contestants.

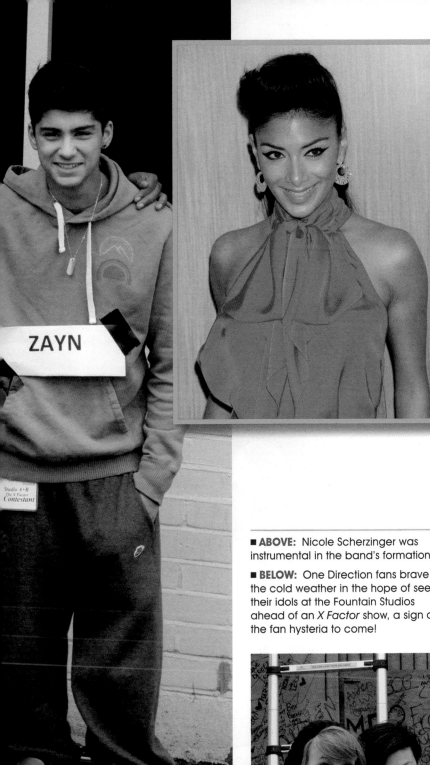

five minutes). The emotional roller coaster came to an end when the five boys agreed to become One Direction!

For Liam it must have been a very tough time and perhaps it was just a little too good to be true. At just 14 years old he had auditioned for the show and had a long wait to walk onto the stage in front of Simon. At the time, Liam thought he had a good chance of making it although now he thinks he wouldn't have been able to handle it if he had. It was also the year of really strong competitors. The acts that made it to the final that year, Alexandra Burke and JLS, went on to great success in the UK and Europe; if he had made it to the live shows he thinks he would probably have left pretty quickly. Liam then went back to school, which was hard. Being on stage had given him the inspiration he needed to be a real pop star! After finding it hard to settle back at school, some advice from a teacher made him realize that he needed to work hard. What if he never became a singer? What if he didn't make it next time? After school, Liam had

■ **ABOVE:** Nicole Scherzinger was instrumental in the band's formation.

■ **BELOW:** One Direction fans brave the cold weather in the hope of seeing their idols at the Fountain Studios ahead of an *X Factor* show, a sign of the fan hysteria to come!

chosen to go to music college and he concentrated on performing in small shows. He worked with quite a lot of people in the music industry but kept his options open so that he could return to audition for *The X Factor*.

Five good-looking boys from across the British Isles had arrived, but they now faced their biggest challenge yet: becoming the best boy band that they could be, and to make it to live shows and the final! Being a solo artist is very different from being in a group. There are so many things to think about from the styles of music that might suit the singers, to who will sing what, how the song will be shared, what they need to do to pull together as performers, as well as how to dance alongside each other. All five boys have good voices, but they are very different too. How could they have just met, form a group and be good enough to go to the live shows? There was a lot of hard work to be done and the boys knew that they had a long way to go to become a group capable of winning *The X Factor.* After forming the group, One Direction spent a week together getting to know each other. There were big ups and downs for Liam on his way to his *X Factor* dream, and because he had always wanted to be a solo artist it was difficult to imagine being in a band with four guys he'd never met before. But it was probably one of the best decisions he ever made.

One Direction were one of eight groups invited to Judges' Houses in Spain. They knew that only three

■ **ABOVE:** Liam had previously auditioned and got as far as Judges' Houses.

■ **LEFT:** Would these five boys be able to work hard enough to make it as a boy band?

■ **ABOVE:** Harry Styles and Louis Tomlinson arrive at the Fountain Studios for *The X Factor*.

■ **ABOVE RIGHT:** Simon Cowell and his former girlfriend/pop star Sinitta helped to push the boys through Judges' Houses.

■ **RIGHT:** One Direction and fellow *X Factor* contestants.

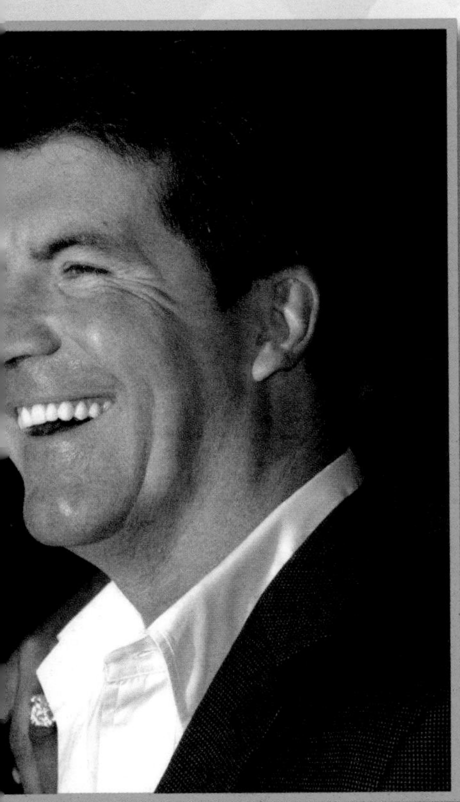

groups would be going through to the live shows and they had a lot to prove to Simon if they were going to be one of them. The boys arrived at the villa in Marbella and made focusing on their formation as a band their only priority. They performed "Torn" by Natalie Imbruglia in a real team effort in front of Simon and his former pop-star protégé Sinitta. Hearing that they'd made it through to the live shows was an amazing experience for the boys who were hungrier than ever for success. They managed to get their act together in just a few short weeks and all the effort, determination, and hard work had paid off. The long working hours had been worth it – they were through!

Live shows were another scary time for the boys. One Direction was now really coming together, but live shows meant just that – they were live. There were 16 acts that made it to the live shows in season seven (usually there are just 12), which made it harder for One Direction. Beginning on October 9, 2010, the live shows took place at The Fountain Studios in Wembley, London, where contestants performed on the Saturday night with the results being revealed on the Sunday night show. One Direction came in fourth in week one and then moved to third place in weeks two and three. They would keep those positions for the whole 10 weeks although this would not be revealed until after

the show when weekly results would be published.

JLS were a great R&B boy band who were runners-up to winner Alexandra Burke in 2008. Although they didn't win the competition, appearing on *The X Factor* made the talented group household names in the UK, bringing boy bands back to the pop world. This was a good thing for One Direction when they made it to the live shows in 2010, but traditionally, groups have never got to the number one position on *The X Factor.* Solo artists had managed to hit the top spot every time on the show and remained popular with the audience and viewers, but JLS changed that when they proved that a group could again make it to the number two position.

Simon Cowell has his critics in the music industry and there are those that don't agree with or like the influence that he has on the pop scene, but he is probably the most influential person to have worked in the industry in recent years. Talent show stars like Leona Lewis, JLS, Cheryl Cole, Alexandra Burke, and One Direction go to show that he has changed the face of the music industry. Critics who include rock stars and journalists think that Simon Cowell was simply someone in the right place at the right time when music was being discovered in a new way. When music began to take off over the Internet rather than through CDs, and social media began to grow, Simon Cowell made Saturday night TV a must. It has led to some very popular music from many different artists and bands, and it has given One Direction the opportunity to make it big!

■ **RIGHT:** One Direction attending a movie premiere during The *X Factor* live shows.

One Direction to World Domination

When One Direction made it to the finals of *The X Factor* they were signed by Simon Cowell's and Sony Music Entertainment's company Syco Entertainment in a £2 million ($3.1 million) deal. Syco has exclusive rights to sign all *X Factor* winners and finalists. This means that Syco looks after the band's music, production, distribution, digital rights, television, and movie content. But, the deal includes other partnerships too and the band is signed to Columbia Records in North America. Pop is a fascinating musical genre because it can have many different influences and can combine ideas from music, fashion, art, books, science, and politics. On the other hand it can be just about a beautiful melody, and good harmonies. Pop does not have to have great meaning. It is also anything that the songwriter and the artist performing want it to be!

BELOW: The boys have had a staggering amount of success in a short time.

Having come third in the competition, the boys had no way of knowing whether Simon would want to work with them any more. In his usual way, Simon gave very little away when he spoke to 1D after the finals show. He had enjoyed working with them and told the boys how good they were. It came as a total shock when he revealed that he wanted to sign the band. But this now meant that One Direction were well and truly on the way to stardom. At the start of 2011, the boys heard that they were destined for the US and were going to record there! Their manager, Richard Griffiths, announced that they would be traveling to LA and recording with RedOne's crew. The band found that they had fans in the US, which came as a great surprise, but they were even more overwhelmed by the fans waiting for them on their return to Heathrow. One Direction LOVE meeting their fans – they are very keen to say "hello" to the fans that wait for them, to the fans that go to see them, and to meet their fans when on tour.

The album "Up All Night" was released on November 18, 2011 in Ireland, and was then released in the UK three days later, although it had to wait until March 13, 2012 for its release in the US. The songs "What Makes You Beautiful" and "One Thing" both did well in the charts. "One Thing" was their highest-peaking single in Australia, while "What Makes You Beautiful," released in 2011, was the band's highest chart-topping single so far when it made it to the #1 spot in the UK. Work on the album began

early in 2011 and includes pop, pop rock, and dance-pop music, while the lyrics concentrate on being young, relationships, and having fun. The band believes that the album is powerful, which fans backed up when it debuted at #2 in the albums chart in the UK and went straight to #1 in the US on Billboard.

The promotion for the debut album was so successful that

Columbia Records had to release it in the US a week early because demand from fans was so high!

There had been a four-month marketing campaign through the use of social media to build up the band's fan base – and guess what – it worked!

Social media has had a big

■ **BELOW:** One Direction get their first taste of a fan frenzy as they arrived in Scotland to promote their debut single "What Makes You Beautiful".

FITCH
NY
197
A&
Fitch
18

part to play in changes to the music industry and the success of bands like One Direction. Today, social networking sites like The Pic-Nic Village, Twitter, Facebook, iTunes, YouTube, and Ping have revolutionized the way music is discovered. Today it is the fans – like you – that decide which music is best, which music is relevant. By letting all your friends know what you like and what you think is good via the Internet, music is shared in a huge way. In today's modern world, the companies and shops selling music face to face now sell it online too. This means that many more people across the world are discovering new music (and bands) much more quickly. This has been good for 1D. It used to be really difficult to make it in the music industry and, although it's still not easy, free digital music that can be released very quickly on the Internet is helping new artists to find fans (which is how they become popular very fast). Social media has been a massive success for One Direction because it has helped the band find dedicated fans. Social media is almost like the new radio! 1D's management team even employ a social media team because distributing music in this way is so powerful. By using social media, the boys are closer and more connected to all their Directioners! Twitter is a big part of life for 1D and the fans. The band can reach their fans on a global scale – and fast – and no other band in the history of music has ever been such a huge success in this way before.

The second album, "Take Me Home," was released on November 12, 2012, following the extremely successful first tour, which gained the band fans in

■ **LEFT:** The boys arrive back from LA into Heathrow Airport to crowds of girls, 2011.

ONE DIRECTION

Oceania and North America. It is estimated that in 2013 the boys will be worth a cool $100 million (£64 million)! This is all thanks to the first album going to #1 in 16 countries and a DVD that topped the charts in 25 countries across the globe. With the second studio album and a world tour in 2013, their continuing success is set to double the boys' overall worth. Simon Cowell was said to have taken an interest in 1D's new material in 2012 and paid the boys a visit while they were working on the new album in June. The album cover shot, released in August, was of the boys climbing all over a telephone box. The first song on the album, "Live While We're Young," comes complete with a dance routine – they worked on two different dances, but only one of them made the video. The excitement about the second album grew as it was confirmed that the boys had made it in America. They won three VMAs: best new artist, best pop video, and most share-worthy video. It saw them celebrating with pal, Justin Bieber, as they toasted their US success – they were the first British act to debut at the top of the album chart Stateside.

Just as "Take Me Home" was released, it was announced that the boys would need to ensure they were fit for the eight-month world tour in 2013! The album had already seen them face a grueling work schedule, but the tour would mean much more hard work. The boys took an active role in the recording process – Niall got to play guitar – and they were delighted to work on collaborations with Ed Sheeran and UK band McFly. The album topped the charts in more than 35 countries, including the

■ **ABOVE:** One Direction perform at Nickelodeon's 25th Annual Kids' Choice Awards in Los Angeles.

■ **FAR LEFT:** One Direction at a public appearance in London where they met fans.

■ **LEFT:** The boys perform on their UK tour.

TODAY
TOYOTA
CONCERT SERIES
TODAY
YAMAHA
MOTIF

EBS

UK, US, Australia, and Canada. It received favorable reviews from critics and helped 1D to sell more than one million copies of two different albums in one calendar year.

It was announced in January 2013 that the boys would be getting their own private jet for the world tour. Dubbed Air Force One Direction, the luxury jumbo meant that the lads could avoid long check-in queues at airports! 2013 will prove to be a bumper year for the boys, who jet all over Europe in the spring, including visits to France, Germany and Spain. The first leg of the tour kicked off at London's O2 Arena on February 22, 2013, with a mammoth 29-date tour of North America following the bands European dates, before 1D jet off to Australia and New Zealand. Meanwhile, in January 2013, the boys dressed in kimonos after landing in Japan – it was 50 years since The Beatles had done the same, but the five lads were greeted in exactly the same way as the fab four – with traditional costume and hundreds of hysterical fans. The boys were in Tokyo to begin work on their 3D movie and to promote the second album.

■ **RIGHT INSET:** Olly Murs – the support act on One Direction's American tour, and fellow *X Factor* UK finalist.

■ **RIGHT:** A store in Paris is besieged by Directioners.

■ **BELOW:** One Direction fans waiting to see the boys perform in Auckland, New Zealand.

■ **ABOVE:** G'Day to One Direction in Sydney, Australia.

■ **ABOVE:** One Direction fans go crazy in New York.

AWARDS
MTV

Harry Styles

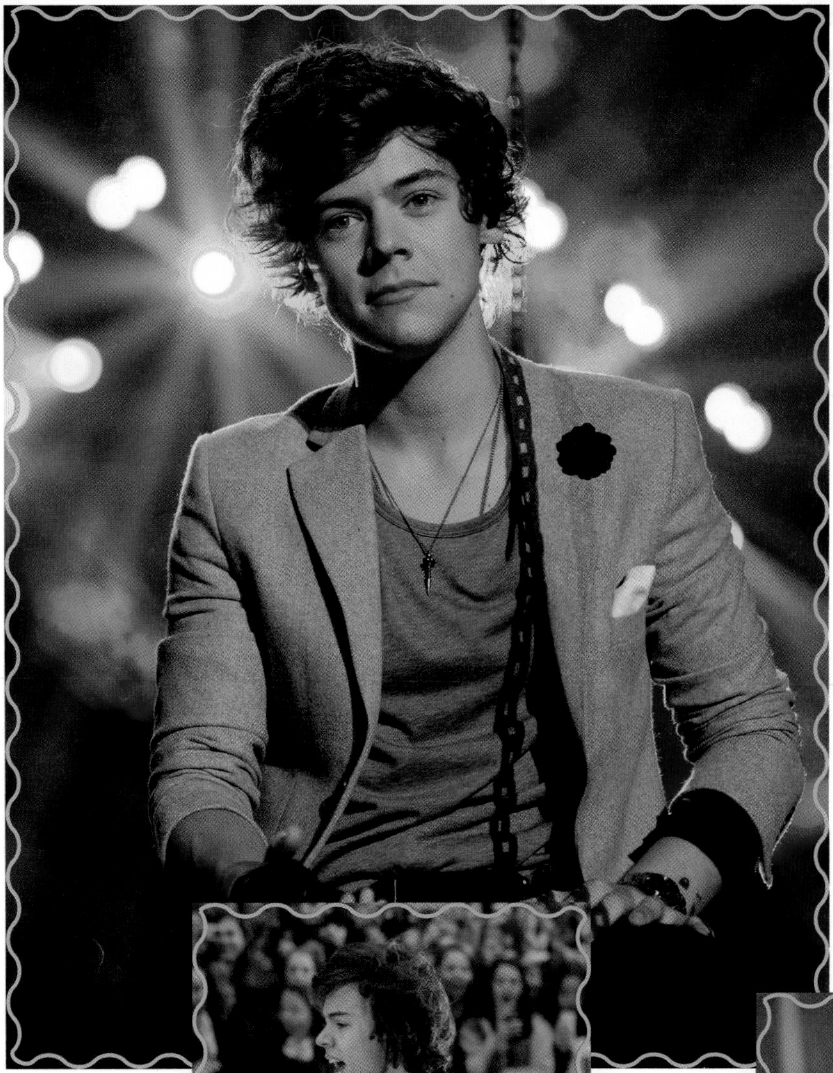

Full name: Harry Edward Styles
Date of birth: February 1, 1994
Place of birth: Evesham, Worcestershire, UK
Star sign: Aquarius
Height: 5 feet 10 inches
Nickname(s): Larry Stylinson (along with band mate Louis Tomlinson) and known as "H" to his family
Parents: Anne Twist and Des Styles
Sibling(s): Older sister Gemma
Ambition(s): Lots of #1s, travel, go back to America, have fun!
Favorite film(s): *Fight Club, Titanic, The Notebook, Love Actually*
Favorite food: Sweetcorn
Favorite fragrance: Blue by Chanel
Favorite artists: Kings of Leon, Coldplay, Foster the People
Biggest musical influences: Elvis Presley, The Beatles, Queen
Best friend(s): Louis Tomlinson
Lives: East London

FACT Files

Zayn Malik

Full name: Zain Jawaad "Zayn" Malik
Date of birth: January 12, 1993
Place of birth: Bradford, UK
Star sign: Capricorn
Height: 5 feet 7 inches
Nickname(s): Zayny Boy, Zayners
Parents: Tricia and Yaser Malik
Sibling(s): Sisters Doniya, Waliyha, and Safaa
Ambition(s): Being given the chance to shine and progress (as a band of course)!
Favorite film(s): *Freedom Writers*
Favorite food: Chicken
Favorite fragrance: Unforgiveable by Sean John
Favorite artists: *NSYNC
Biggest musical influences: Urban music, R&B, rap
Best friend(s): Liam Payne and former drama friends, Danny and Anthony
Lives: London, UK

FACT Files

Liam Payne

Full name: Liam James Payne
Date of birth: August 29, 1993
Place of birth: Wolverhampton, West Midlands, UK
Star sign: Virgo
Height: 5 feet 9 inches
Nickname(s): Li-Li, Liamy, Paynee
Parents: Karen and Geoff Payne
Sibling(s): Older sisters, Ruth and Nicola
Ambition(s): Loving what he's doing with his band mates and not letting the moments pass by...
Favorite film(s): *Toy Story* and *Click*
Favorite food: Chocolate
Favorite fragrance: One Million by Paco Rabanne
Favorite artists: Leona Lewis
Biggest musical influences: Justin Timberlake, Gary Barlow
Best friend(s): Ronnie, Martin, and Andy
Lives: Birmingham

FACT
Files

Louis Tomlinson

Full name: Louis William Tomlinson

Date of birth: December 24, 1991

Place of birth: Doncaster, South Yorkshire, UK

Star sign: Capricorn

Height: 5 feet 9 inches

Nickname(s): Larry Stylinson (because of close friendship with Harry Styles), and Tommo

Parents: Johanna Tomlinson and Mark Tomlinson

Sibling(s): Younger sisters Charlotte, Félicité, Daisy, and Phoebe

Ambition(s): For the band to take over the world!

Favorite film(s): *Grease*

Favorite food: Pasta and pizza

Favorite fragrance: Doesn't have one!

Favorite artists: Adele and The Fray

Biggest musical influences: Robbie Williams – Louis met his idol on *The X Factor* in 2010. He is also influenced – big time – by Michael Jackson

Best friend(s): Harry Styles and Stan

Lives: Doncaster

FACT Files

Niall Horan

Full name: Niall James Horan
Date of birth: September 13, 1993
Place of birth: Mullingar, County Westmeath, Republic of Ireland
Star sign: Virgo
Height: 5 feet 7 inches
Nickname(s): Nialler
Parents: Maura Horan and Bobby Horan
Sibling(s): Older brother Greg
Ambition(s): For the band to get bigger, better, and stronger!
Favorite film(s): *The Godfather*, *Grease*, and *Goodfellas*
Favorite food: Pizza
Favorite fragrance: Armani Mania
Favorite artists: The Script, The Eagles, The Kooks, The Doors, Michael Bublé
Biggest musical influences: Ed Sheeran, The Eagles, The Script, Bon Jovi
Best friend(s): Dillan, Brad, Sean, and Scott
Lives: Ireland

FACT Files

On the Road and on Tour

After selling 12 million records, scooping a number of prestigious awards, entertaining the world at the Olympic Closing Ceremony, and taking America by storm, it was time for the boys to reach out once more. Their debut single and the subsequent album had assured the boys of success, and there was no stopping them, with help from their dedicated fan base, including celebs like Justin Bieber, Katy Perry, and Rihanna. (US First Lady, Michelle Obama, is a huge fan and invited the boys to the White House…)

"We know we are living the dream," stated Niall in an interview in September 2012, "but I don't know if it will ever sink in." In March 2012, 1D made their first trip Stateside where they performed at the Nickelodeon Kids' Choice Awards. By September, they had picked up three gongs at the MTV Video Music Awards (VMA) and signed an $11 million deal to be the new faces of Pepsi. "Live While We're Young," the single from the second album, came out at the end of the month and the band really did have it all. The song was the fastest-selling pre-order single

■ **ABOVE:** One Direction arrive at Nickelodeon's 25th Annual Kids' Choice Awards, in Los Angeles, California, March 2012.

■ **BELOW:** Harry walks on stage to accept the best pop video award for "What Makes You Beautiful" at the MTV Video Music Awards, September 2012.

in history and topped the charts in 40 countries including Australia, France, Spain, Brazil, and the UK. Helped by creative director of Syco, Tim Byrne, social marketing on Tumblr, YouTube, Facebook, and Twitter played a big part in the band's rise and continued success. Connecting directly with the fans has had a massive impact. There are more than six million followers on Twitter, both for the boys collectively and as individuals. Nothing like this has ever been seen before!

So, what next? A world tour of course... The tour got underway in February 2013 with more than 100 shows planned in the US, the UK, Ireland, and Australasia. In the UK, the O2 Arena had six dates sold out within hours and more than 300,000 tickets were sold in a day. Due to huge demand, extra dates were added for the North American leg of the tour and more than $15.5 million (£10 million) in ticket sales was reported in Australia and New Zealand.

The tour was spectacular and, to ensure that it was as exciting as possible, the band asked Dynamo to become involved in the production. It was Dynamo's job to provide the "wow" factor. Steven Frayne – aka Dynamo – had already impressed the boys with his walk on water across the Thames in London and his levitating tricks. At the time the tour was announced, the acoustic song, "Little Things," written by Ed Sheeran, was tipped to be their best single *ever*! Released in November 2012 on the album "Take Me Home," it was first

■ **ABOVE:** The boys pictured during the filming of a Pepsi commercial in New Orleans.

■ **BELOW:** Fans of the band have been responsible for their huge worldwide success; these fans in Milan go wild for the boys!

posted on YouTube to the delight of fans. But, there was still a lot of work to do…

The tour started in February and lasted eight months, so the boys needed to make sure they were fit before it started. Unfortunately, the band had been plagued by injuries. Niall's knee had dislocated a number of times, Liam had broken his toe, Harry was suffering from a bad back, and Zayn was on crutches having hurt himself out partying. The boys' management decided to help them get in shape by organizing Pilates for Harry and banning Niall from playing soccer. They also had to cut down on all the fast food that they'd enjoyed while recording their second album. By this time, the band had become the first group to reach number 1 in the US with their debut album, and "Take Me Home" was setting the scene for superstardom. Niall played guitar on a number of songs on the album and 1D collaborated with some of their heroes, including Ed Sheeran and McFly.

Just before the tour got underway, the boys were back in the United States where they were watched by a 200-strong group of One Directioners waiting for a glimpse of their idols while they stayed at the Trump International Hotel opposite Central Park. The reason for the visit was for 1D to play at Madison Square Garden in the gig of a lifetime. In January 2013, they made a trip to Ghana in Africa where they became ambassadors for the UK charity Comic Relief. They met local families who benefit from the charity's work and were moved by the poverty they witnessed. To help boost proceeds for Red Nose Day – the charity's major fundraising event – the band released their recording of Blondie's "One Way Or Another" with footage from their trip to Accra in Ghana. There was also time to add their support to the launch of Enough Food for Everyone IF Campaign, where more than 100

■ **ABOVE:** One Direction on stage during the 2012 Capital FM Jingle Bell Ball at the O2 Arena, London.

15175
15675
TEENAGE
KICKS
INSERT COIN
UP TO 5 CAN PLAY

organizations joined forces to tackle global hunger. 1D followed this with a trip to Tokyo in Japan where they wore kimonos to celebrate their visit. It was here that work began on their eagerly awaited 3D movie (as well as promoting their second album of course).

There was no sign by the beginning of February 2013 that the excitement was waning. The boys were given their own jet for the world tour, complete with 1D branding on the tail! The luxury jumbo, which cost $4.6 million (£3 million), was dubbed Air Force One Direction and meant that long check-in queues could be avoided for the European leg of the tour across France, Spain, and Germany. The jumbo then took the boys to North America – they had two of the top six records in the US in 2012 ("Up All Night" and "Take Me Home") where they started a 29-date stint before heading for Australasia. Filming of the 3D movie continued into February prior to the Take Me Home tour and, by the end of the month, the hardest working boys in pop were given their own personal assistants. The assistants were all chosen by the boys themselves and added to the 90-strong team that look after them including managers, publicists, and newly appointed financial advisers. It was essential that for the world tour, the band mates were all as organized as possible!

Having won the Global Success gong at the Brit Awards in late February, the boys were all ready for their world tour. The first night got underway at the O2 Arena in London on Saturday, February 23. The Take Me Home tour was on the road, at last, where reportedly some tickets changed hands for up to £5,000. It was an exciting start to the eight-month tour. A big black curtain was drawn across the stage and then dropped to reveal musicians in place, already playing their instruments. Zayn was among the group on stage and was joined, one by one, by his fellow band members. The show opened with "Up All Night," in front of a "hungry" crowd who

■ **ABOVE:** 1D perform on stage during the BRIT Awards 2013 at the O2 Arena.

■ **ABOVE RIGHT:** The boys kicked off their 2013 World Tour in February 2013; the O2 Arena in London had six dates sold out within hours and over 300,000 tickets sold in one day!

■ **LEFT:** The boys pictured signing their Hasbro doll lookalikes at a press event in New York.

■ **ABOVE:** The boys perform at Madison Square Garden in New York.

■ **LEFT:** Japanese actress Maki Horikita, poses with the band.

■ **RIGHT:** The boys showing off the kimonos they were presented with at the airport in Japan.

enthusiastically waved thousands of banners at their idols. Costume changes were covered by videos of 1D being the charismatic band that One Directioners adore. The show also included a platform that moved out above the audience. The performance ended, before an excited crowd, with four of the boys jumping through holes that opened at the front of the stage. Harry walked off stage to thunderous applause and a great deal of excitement from the fans.

The show included all the songs from the two albums amid deafening screams from the fans, who thought the gig was amazing. For many fans, it was: "The best night ever…"

During the tour, the boys were accompanied by chef Sarah Nicholas, from Sarah's Kitchen, to cook up tasty meals to sustain them through their schedule. On the menu was uber-healthy food – which included healthier versions of all their favorite foods, especially Mexican dishes. The boys were treated to organic produce and the menu was designed to ensure that they ate properly while away on tour. Fruit and vegetables were high on the list and helped to keep the guys healthy. Smoothies were a firm favorite and orange juice was a must to keep colds at bay.

While rehearsing on tour, audio tracks of screaming girls were played to help give the boys a more authentic experience while carrying out sound checks.

The tour was a commercial success for the band, and included dates from February 23 to November 3, 2013, as the tour was extended to include two dates in Japan following the final show in Melbourne at the end of October. An additional date was added at the O2 Arena in London on April 6, where the boys were filmed for

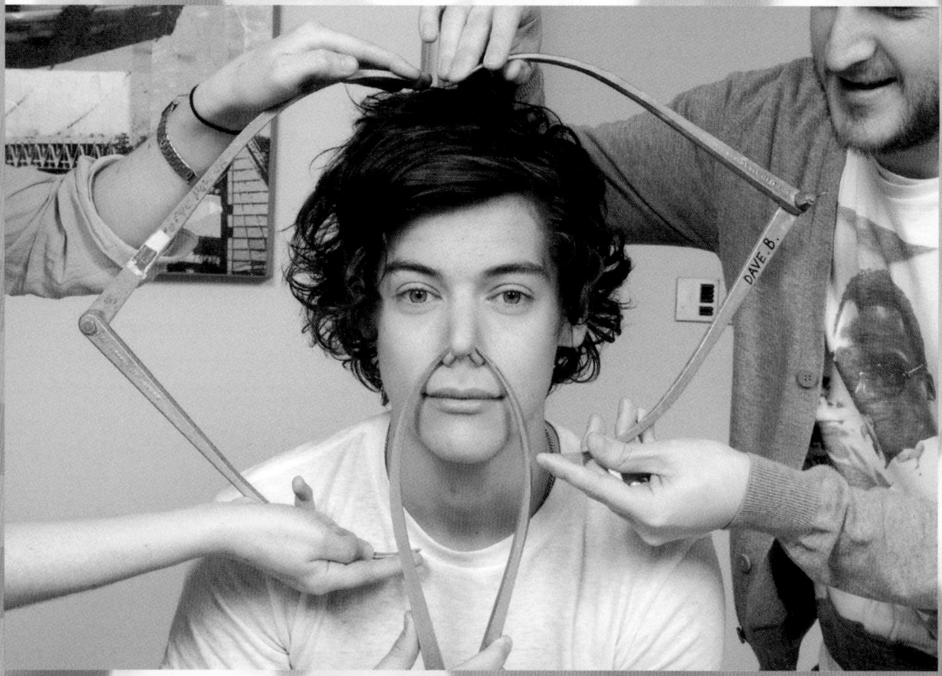

1D – The Movie, which includes footage of the band mates doing everyday things. The additional date began with support acts Camryn and 5sos before the five members of 1D took to the stage. Fans were rewarded by all the band's famous hits and were thanked for their support a number of times before the boys finished with "What Makes You Beautiful." Fans were well impressed with an exciting night of pop, including Niall serenading the appreciative audience with his guitar.

As a pop group, One Direction is one of the best – if not the best according to Directioners across

■ **ABOVE:** Harry Styles has fun during the sculpting process of his wax figure, in which hundreds of precise measurements were taken, ahead of the kick-off of the band's wax figure tour at Madame Tussauds in London, April 2013. The band would then travel to New York, then on to Sydney later in the year.

■ **BELOW:** Wax models of the boys are unveiled at Madame Tussauds in London, April 2013.

the globe. Their rise to fame and their international breakthrough have been swift and staggering. Social networking has helped to create and sustain the group's success, but the band is well aware that the fan base is what keeps them going. An eight-month tour might be tough for the boys, but given the adoration they face night after night, it must surely all be worth it? During the summer of 2013, the boys made two major announcements. First they told their fans they were treating them to a stadium tour in 2014 and then they announced that there would be an official book, with the title *Where We Are: Our Band, Our Story.* The phenomenal story of 1D, charting the band's dreams, aspirations, and their journey so far, will be available for Christmas 2013. So how about that extra tour? The Where We Are tour, made headlines on May 16, 2013 as the boys' new stadium tour in 2014 was unveiled. Dates have been decided, but more are to follow. The first gig on the stadium tour is on April 25, 2014 in Bogatá, while the 13th date to be announced is June 7 at London's Wembley Stadium. Fans went mad on Twitter when the tour was announced, clocking up an impressive million tweets in just 80 minutes!

Five talented boys, with a common dream to make it to the top in the music industry, are reaching the stars; the story is set to continue…

■ **ABOVE:** Cardboard cut-outs of One Direction band members are on display at a pop-up shop.

■ **BELOW:** The boys are poised for more success with the release of their 3D movie and a new album.

Quotes and Trivia

Quotes

"It's important to be yourself and be happy with who you are because that's what makes you unique."

Zayn

"Live life for the moment, because everything else is uncertain."

Louis

"When I was little… I wanted a brother, and now it's like having four of them."

Liam

"If it were legal, I'd marry food."

Niall

"Don't choose the one who is beautiful to the world… choose the one who makes your world beautiful."

Harry

"So crazy to think that we have only known each other two years. It's been so amazing and we have got to do so many amazing things all thanks to each and every one of you guys. It's all gone by so quickly but I'm sure we will have many, many more times to come."

1D

"We have the cutest fan base ever."

1D

"Words will be words, till you bring them to life."

1D

"Every now and then you have like a realization moment where you get goose-bumps and think: I'm literally the luckiest person in the world."

Niall

"Dreams are like stars – you may never touch them, but if you follow them, they will lead you to your destiny."

Liam

"We have a choice… to live, or to exist."

Harry

"Life's a funny thing; the minute you think you've got everything figured, something comes along and turns it all upside down."

Zayn

"Being single doesn't mean that you're weak – it means that you're strong enough to wait for what you deserve."

Niall

"Things change, people change, but you will always be you, so stay true to yourself and never sacrifice who you are for anyone."

Zayn

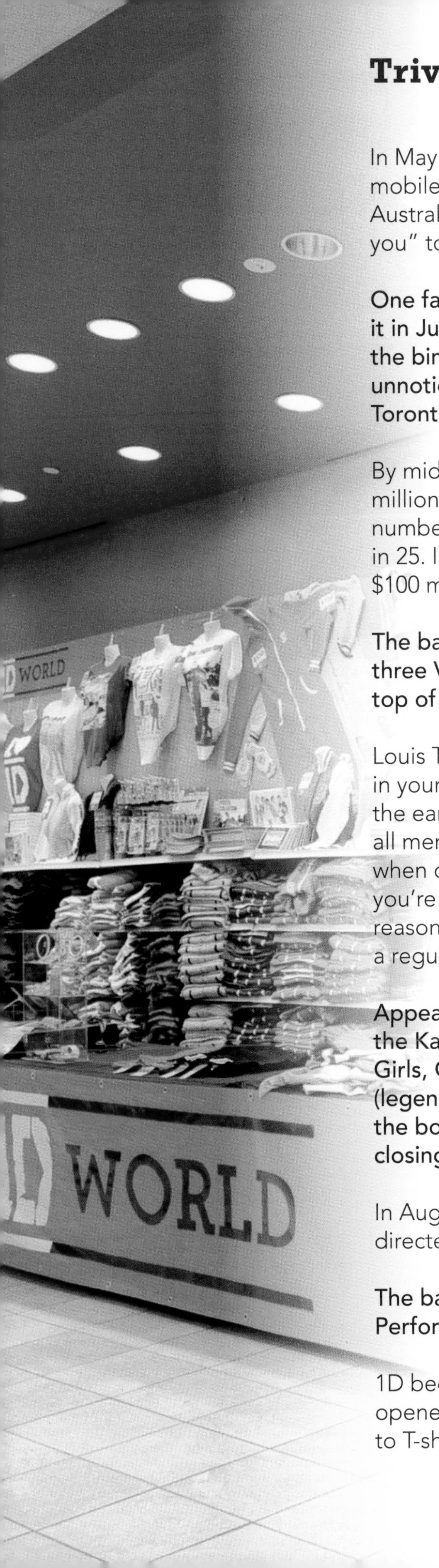

Trivia

In May 2012, the boys faced a whopping $21,400 (£14,000) in mobile telephone bills while on tour in North America and Australia, but Simon Cowell picked up the bill as a "thank you" to the band to celebrate their success.

One fan had to be removed from a dustbin after hiding in it in June 2012, hopeful of seeing their idols. They hid in the bin in an attempt to creep in through a back entrance unnoticed, while another keen fan kayaked across a lake in Toronto to get close while the boys were staying there.

By mid-2012, 1D were reported to be worth a cool $49.7 million (£32 million) thanks to their album that went to number 1 in 16 countries and a DVD that topped the charts in 25. In 2013 the boys' wealth escalated to a staggering $100 million (£64 million).

The band enjoyed great success in the US in 2012 and won three VMAs – they were the first British act to debut at the top of the album chart Stateside.

Louis Tomlinson suffers from tinnitus – a common problem in young musicians that means a persistent buzzing in the ear – and is partially deaf in his right ear. As a result, all members of 1D now wear hi-tech protective earpieces when on stage and during rehearsals. Remember, when you're listening to music on your iPod, keep the volume at a reasonable level at all times. Listening to very loud music on a regular basis can lead to tinnitus and permanent deafness.

Appearing alongside Emeli Sande, Ed Sheeran, Muse, the Kaiser Chiefs, David Bowie, The Who, The Spice Girls, Queen, Elbow, George Michael, Ray Davies (legend from the Kinks), and Jessie J, among others, the boys performed at the London 2012 Olympics' closing ceremony.

In August 2013, the band starred in their very own 3D movie directed by *Super Size Me*'s Morgan Spurlock.

The band performed at the 100th Royal Variety Performance in London in December 2012.

1D became shop idols in New York when a pop-up store opened selling everything from life-sized cardboard cutouts to T-shirts and earrings.

Quick Quiz

(Answers below)

1. How many records have 1D sold?
2. Which ceremony did the band sing at?
3. How much was 1D's mobile phone bill?
4. How many Royal Variety Performances have there been?
5. How much are the boys worth?
6. Who wrote "Little Things"?
7. On which TV show did the boys meet?
8. What kind of box features on their follow-up album?
9. How many VMAs have 1D won?
10. What's wrong with Louis' ears?
11. Who is director of the band's 3D movie?
12. Where is the 1D shop?
13. Who invited the boys to the White House?
14. Which fizzy drink do the boys endorse?
15. Who helped in the production of 1D's first world tour?
16. Before the tour, what did the bosses want?
17. Where did the boys stay in New York?
18. What's Air Force One Direction?
19. What did the boys wear in Japan?
20. Where did 1D go as charity ambassadors?

1, 12 million **2,** Olympics – London 2012 **3,** $21,400 (£14,000) **4,** 100 **5,** $100 million or £64 million **6,** Ed Sheeran **7,** *The X Factor* **8,** A telephone box **9,** Three **10,** He suffers from tinnitus **11,** Morgan Spurlock **12,** New York **13,** First Lady, Michelle Obama **14,** Pepsi **15,** Dynamo **16,** For the boys to get fit **17,** Trump International Hotel **18,** A private jet **19,** Kimonos **20,** Ghana, Africa